MOMENTS IN TIME
Poems of Grief and Healing

Andrea Walker-Williamson

CREATE NOISE PUBLISHING
LOS ANGELES CALIFORNIA

Moments in Time: Poems of Grief and Healing
Copyright © 2016 by Andrea L. Walker-Williamson
Los Angeles, California

All rights reserved
Printed and Bound in the United States of America
September 2016

Published and distributed by Create Noise Publishing
Los Angeles, California
Createnoise1@gmail.com

Cover illustrator: Eli Ziv

Cover Design, Interior Design and Typesetting: Caldonia Joyce

ISBN: 978-0-9961346-4-4

No part of this book may be reproduced, stored in a retrieval system or transmitted in any form or by any means without prior written permission of the publisher—except by a reviewer who may quote brief passages in a review to be printed in a newspaper, magazine or journal.

For inquiries contact: createnoise1@gmail.com

FOREWORD

FOREWORD BY
IESHA BRYANT
CEO/FOUNDER
BERT'S GRANDDAUGHTER'S PLACE

Sometimes we cross paths in pain...

Meeting through hurt...
Connecting with someone who too share stories of a lost love....
As Mrs. Andrea Walker dedicates this book of poetry to her beloved late husband...
I pray this book reaches you right in the midst of what you're going through...
To let you know it's not just you this is happening to....

GOD will give you the strength and you will gain a greater love and appreciate life & your purpose....

In pain we live through them for you, me, us & most importantly (them)....
I believe through pain we learn to live & love deeper even when it hurts.

TABLE OF CONTENTS

FOREWORD 3

PRELUDE 7

FINDING A PATH FOR THE JOURNEY 9
   There is life after death 9
   Until we meet again.... 10
   Searching 11
   Alone 12
   Willing 13
   Other side. 14
   Never die 15
   No Fear 16
   You 17
   Wish. 18

PLACING BURDENS ON WINGS IN THE WIND. 19
   Sleep. 19
   Crushed Flower 20
   Forever 22
   Source. 23
   Closed Windows. 24
   I told you to leave .25
   He Prays 27
   Aren't I woman? 28
   Tired. 30
   Love lost 31
   Love 32

    Will I?..33
    Free..34

CONFESS IT IN TEARFUL VOICES......................35
    Didn't Know.....................................35
    Ashamed...36
    Why do they always leave me?....................37
    Forever...39
    I cried...40

TO BATHE MY SOUL IN MUDDY WATERS..................41
    The Candle......................................41
    Dark man..44
    Stain...45
    The beauty of a lie.............................46

LOVE IS LIBERATING................................47
    His Smile.......................................47
    My Flower.......................................48
    Heart...49
    His...50
    Love It...51
    Friend..52
    Family..53
    Grandma...54
    Gain..55
    Man...56
    Our lives.......................................57
    Love is like the sea............................58
    The Rose..59
    Beside You......................................60
    This Race.......................................61

PRELUDE

Grief takes you through so many emotions. This book of poetry explores those emotions.

For my family and the numerous hearts that have bonded with mine. I have learned that love really does liberate.

This book of poetry and expressions is a tribute to my beloved husband, Terrance Schmichael Williamson October 14, 1979- December 8, 2015. This is also in homage to the many we have lost:

Lashawn Duke, Donald Charles Young, Emmanuel Ray Young, Virginia Young, Jamie Walker, Marquice Little, Ella Williamson, Allen Thomas, Nekaron Lawson and Doretha Smith.

FINDING A PATH FOR THE JOURNEY

There is life after death

Beauty that hides behind the hollow wood, that builds a fortress in the forest.

Pain that breaths life into my lips one echo at a time.

As I lick my wounds I am reminded that I am alive to feel them.

The grass is still thick, green and full. I can see colors, identify rainbows, stretch my arms wide and collect hugs from those who love me. I hear sounds. Witness the echoes of instruments in the distance fighting for the encore.

There is life after the pain, after the sorrow. When the tears have dried and the eyes remain puffy, heavy and sad.

There is life to carry us into the realm of peace. Where we can identify the memories and release some of the weight that we captured from our loss.

The tears escape so freely, but let them. They allow you to weep. At your request we can share thoughts, experiences, discussions and the mission at hand.

Life has to continue although we have left some force in a realm unknown.

> Blow into your hands.
> Hold them close.
> What do you feel?

Can you feel the air between your fingers? Can you feel air—life?

That is your gift.

Until we meet again...

Can't take it.

Walking past your car in the driveway.

Sliding past your shoes in the hallway.

Glancing at your pictures as your eyes meet mine.

I can still hear you, smell you and feel your presence in our room at night.

The wrinkled pillowcase still represents the space you claimed in our bed.

My dry tired eyes wait in the dark for you to rollover and slide to my side.

The television continues to record your favorite shows and Sunday mornings still echo you calling Pops to discuss the football lineup.

The kids continue to rush into our room looking for a tireless battle royale, until you turn them upside-down and wait for them to tap out one-by-one.

The stereo continues to play your favorite Pandora mix and I smile as each song takes my mind to a different time.

I just can't take it but I love the peace that surrounds your memories.

I stare at the pictures that you once refused to take and I'm thankful for the persistence that I had to force you to pose oftentimes.

The past was incredible but the future brings uncertainty, as the journey without your physical form seems so different. Difficult, but I must go on until we meet again....

Searching

Searching
Not sure what's wrong.
Don't know what I'm missing.
Crying, feel like I'm dying.
This distance feels depressing.

Can't be explained,
They fight to figure me out.
My thoughts are too advanced for them.
They aren't sure, what I'm about.
I'm alone, still surrounded by people,
I'm innocent; they're doing what's illegal.

I came here searching.
Searching for something better,
Something wonderful and true.
I saw a light. I saw a glow.

I saw something different that was set in stone.
I don't know what I'm doing
Sometimes …not sure where I'm going.
At times I just think.
How scary it has been,
Not knowing…

Alone

Alone,
No. Walking with him.
Single—No. Married to him.
Traveling alone,
Shadow beside me,
Maybe this shadow is a transcendent image of my father.

Maybe his spirit is directly connected with mine and I can see him,
As I walk on by.

Maybe my physical being is not as bound as his,
But I live in the same, image of him.
My faith can't be touched.

Belief helps me conquer just as much.
Won't attempt to tread so thin, now that I know he died for
    my sins.

This absolute being makes me whole,
Survive in his likeness. Consummate my soul.
His image or mere likeness of me?
A shadow is all that you see.
What does that thin, dark form create in your eyes?
All that he is dwells in the heart, body and mind.

Willing

Walls caving in,
Doors breaking down.
It's going to take alot before my feet will touch the ground.
Feels like, I'm bound by my hands.
Something's glued to my feet.
Still nothing can stop me.
I can't be broken from fear of defeat!
Body is hurting.

Thoughts are on the race.
Can't be still, its as if someone has taken my place.
Not sure what's come over me.
Experiencing is all that I know.
I am a teachable person,
Willing to learn what I don't know.

Other side

Afraid to say goodbye.
Alone,
Don't know the reasons why.
Sit back and watch you die.
Can't do much,
Sometimes I cry.
I try to pretend. It'll never end.
Thought it was the beginning.
Why treat it, like it's the end?
I cherish you.
I give you my word.
Please believe in me, it can work.
Don't leave us.
Were all we have in this cruel world.
Just don't give up.
Don't say goodbye,
In my mind, you're still alive.
Your spirit hasn't died.
Do what you can before you reach—the other side.

Never die

Never die.
You entered my thoughts,
Escaped that other world.
Filled my spirit with happiness, encouraged me to continue.
Granted me access into your heart.
Spread your wings apart.
You are my angel.
I love the way you think.
It's you that I dream of, as I sleep.
You roam through my mind,
Comfort me when I cry.
If such love continues,
I will never die.

No Fear

Eyes close to escape the trouble.
Rest and release in search of more muscle.
Runaway in my dreams.
Supplement my past for my future.
In the darkness I hide from what's actually there.
Freeze time, turn away from what faces me.
My reality has no fear.

You

We share each other's breath,
Expose each other's spots.
Breath calm and cool,
Share each other's thoughts.
I curve to you as you curve to me.
Did some things that made you scream.
There was fire in your eyes,
Intensity in your spirit
Knowledge of pain and hurt caused me to fear it.
Eyes closed, wounds open,
You made me want it.

Self-sacrificing, giving yourself up.
There is never enough.
A simple smirk, a little smile
Makes me feel—this moment, is worth my while.
Smooth and slick we slide together.
Something this good must last forever.
There's more for me to say, more for me to do.

Wish

Wish I had a poem to read you, a song to sing to you.
A cake to bring you—
Food to feed you, some way to greet you.

Instead, I need you! Wish we could borrow you, for a few years more.

To enjoy your spirit, embrace the heart you tamed.
Blink and see the very vision of your face.

Perhaps we were spoiled…always had you close.
At arms length, a phone call away.

Come to realize that we wont see you in the physical sense on this earth again.

Be waiting for the day that we'll meet again.
There I know that you aren't alone.

Arms are all around you. They have welcomed you home.

PLACING BURDENS ON WINGS IN THE WIND

Sleep

Am I asleep when I dream?
Do I dream what I'm to see?
With so much going on, I can't write it all down.
Wish I were asleep.
When I sleep, I'm really free.

Crushed Flower

There's nothing worse than a crushed flower. So many pedals folded over, dancing with color.

Noticeably valuable, its signature within each line.
Prose attempts to describe its nature.

Unsure if she acknowledges her purpose with the pieces she has missing.

Separated from her birth state, she appears strong, relentless, and daring.

Her voice cries out and echoes the courage and strength we know nothing of.

She appears to be unaware, representing so many things.
Saving us from ourselves, lighting our path.
Allowing us one last attempt to be closer to God in his embrace.

Broken, she continues to live.
Her ability to grow is not captured nor is it lost…

For she lives for others—and not for herself.
Crushed, she sits alone among others like her, striped away of her outer coat.

Sending a message with her appearance.

Transporting information to all social strata in the most
   common language ever spoken. Without words, she still
   has a voice linking continuous expression accessible to all.

She has no choice but to convey, preserve and stimulate.

Though damaged, she appears WHOLE.

We know not, when she is hurt. Her cries left unheard.
The quality of her beaten being does not exist in her mind.

For her innovation is not of our understanding.
No one doubts her efficacy.

We must preserve her origin; instead we take it for granted.

So accustomed to the myths…

To the intellectual climate of our own lives we do not realize
   she is the beginning of ours.

These traditional forms are pointed in the direction beyond
   our reach.

She cannot share all that she knows.

Perhaps someone will appreciate her art—her form, her being,
   before she is no longer.

Forever

Forever in your debt,
Forever in your shadow.
You've already won half the battle.
Never will I forsake you.
Don't ever plan to hurt you.
Emotions under control.
I still want you.
Can't live for you.
Afraid to abuse you.
On my knees at night,
Praying that I'd never lose you.
You dwell in my heart,
Stay on my mind.
Memories that forever connect.
Our souls enter-twine.

Source

Innocent and sexual.
You exposed your soul to me.
The look in your eyes was a turn on for me.
Your lips,
So sensual with depth.
I was so aroused,
You nearly took my breath.
Your movement was rhythmic; your body is slick.
 I gravitate towards you.
A feeling this good is not temporary.
Lust is an intense desire, but even in your absence,
I have this craving, this fire.
The pleasure that I gain is a result of the excitement,
That makes me go insane.
Come to me, feel my elegance, strip me of my force.
My thoughts are married to you.
 I will reach for the center.
Your heart is my source.

Closed Windows

Closed windows.
Closed windowpanes.
Fogged mirrors,
Battered shades,
Cracked walls,
Urinated stalls,
No cushion to break my fall.
Horizons with,
No solid background for me.
Wrecked dreams,
Destroyed with no mercy.
Inferno with no air.
My soul must be saved.
Uninterrupted— power of the night.
Open a window so my spirit can take flight.

I told you to leave

I remember when I told you to leave.
Gave you permission to go!

I told you to pack your bags and I would be fine because I
 didn't want you to know—

To know how much you mean to me.
 The many ways… that I could never fully explain.

That you made me whole.
I knew you were my second half.

The bitter piece that I struggled with, didn't want to love
 anything or anyone that much.
You would laugh when I was angry.

You said you felt that I didn't mean to say the things that I had said.

The funny thing is that I knew you would never pack up with
 intentions to move on.

I felt that you were with me in your heart and with your words.

The way you celebrated all your events, I knew them first!

It was in how gracious you would brush at my hair.
How much time you dedicated to taking down my braids.

How great you were at massaging the pain from my back.

There were months of appointments where you sat alongside me.

You took notes while with the doctors and you would often monitor me. It was then that I was sure that you could never go.

But still I would scold you and push you out the door.
You just laughed and went to bed.
You said I would feel better tomorrow.
I remember when I told you to leave.
Gave you permission to go.

I nodded my head and ignored you for days.
I wanted to believe it because you had made me hurt inside.

I felt this warmth surrounding my heart and it was when I thought of you that forced me to forgive you.
You never left but I tired to force you out.

The worst feeling is when the door can swing either way and it leaves room for self-doubt.

I have these memories of telling you to follow your heart and you would ball up beside me.

I wanted to be angry but I loved you even more.
I told you to leave.

However, I always wanted you to stay.
How I sit and reflect on those days.

He Prays

There's truth in his smile,
Honesty in his eyes.

His lips give birth to a sonnet unknown to man.
The sag of his pants represent what most don't understand.

He's often confused of being harder than he is.
For you do not give power to material that others use to
   strengthen them.

His hands carry many burdens for no one understands.

His heavy feet enforce the steps that he makes.

He is mental, taking on the troubles of the world.
Everything, in his possession has a purpose.
The more he tries, the harder life becomes.

He shows love to his brothers,
There's familiarity in their greetings,
For, he knows their struggle.

His prayers reach heaven faster than ours.
He tries to please his family.
Struggles to keep meals in his home.
Brings with him, unique gifts of love, tradition and hope.

He's a broken man, who couldn't escape the pain.
Works his son harder than normal, wants the best for him.
   Wants his babies to have more than he did.

Sleepless nights repeat themselves night after night.
His head- aches during the day. He knows nothing but his family.

This is why he prays.

Aren't I woman?

Aren't I woman? Strong, yet fragile.
Made from God just as all mankind.
I die when I give birth to humanity,
Forever caring and nurturing those around me.

Aren't I woman? With the ability to sense your body language, read your expressions and connect to you mentally. My intuitive nature makes me a psychic yet my naïve innocence gives me appeal. You can notice me in a dark room. I can carry the burdens of others but I could never relate the baggage of my own past.

Aren't I woman with curves out of this world? My dreams go beyond the minds of anyone who is limited with the belief that I will discount my journey because of my gender. When I, in fact seek to go further because my determination will not allow my mind to comprehend giving up!

Aren't I a woman seeking the reduction in oppression that poses a threat to my family, to our growth yet I cry tears of joy as I climb out the madness fighting those who pretend and with systematic structure they intend to keep my children down!

Aren't I woman? Mother of many, and owner of none.
I am mother Africa. My horn is great, can you hear me in your soul?

My intuition leads me to many nations collecting my offspring to remind them where they originated. I only know love.

For my awareness often causes me to fear the one thing that can divide my babies from one another.

For even Satan had to ask God for permission to touch Job. My motherly instincts have led me to touch the faces of my enemies and to allow them to understand what my fears are.

Aren't I woman? Strong with a beating heart, a warm hand and a heavy bosom! Aren't I the nurse who healed your wounds and cared for your bruises?

Aren't I the lawyer that was allowed to represent you and to stand before the judge when you were locked away, hidden and afraid? Aren't I woman? Searching in the darkness, wandering with a limited light source.

Beaten and battered, I make my way down a path because I am sure the journey will not end this way.
I am still woman. As I proceed to take my seat, I sit across the table of the Heavenly Father and I answer when he calls out to me.

I heard my name and all that I represent, a strong woman!

Tired

She said that she was leaving.
Tired of hurting.
Fear— of the pain.
Meds weren't helping,
Slowly driving her insane.
Closed her eyes,
Never did she wake again.

Tired of trying to continue,
In a fight, that was not meant for her to win.

Tired of searching for respect,
Peace of mind and a better tomorrow.
No longer accepting less,
She realized that she must rest.
That her time — was borrowed.

Love lost

Loving you. You're so far away.

Loving you,
Still can't see you today.
Loving you,
Still see visions of your face.
Loving you,
No one can take your place.
Loving you,
So easy for me to do.
Loving you,
When you're gone, my heart is hungry for you.
Loving you,
With every fiber in my body.
Loving you,
My heart pumped fast as we parted.
Loving you,
And I always will.
Loving you,
I know how it feels.

Love

You entered my thoughts,
Escaped to that other world.
Filled my spirit with happiness, encouraged me to continue.
Granted me access into your heart.
Now spread your wings apart.
You are my agent.
I love the way you think.
It's you that I dream of, as I sleep.
You roam through my mind.
Comfort me when I cry.
 If such love continues, you will never die.

Will I?

Will I be defeated?
Will I win?
Who will knock me out?

If I turn over please leave my body on the poetic pages of the book of David.

The words that have reached out and took my grandmother hostage.

Words that are memorized and stored in our hearts.
What must I do to be placed on the very words that have affected so many?

Will God create a special corner just for me?
Will he speak in a passionate voice that calms the rivers?

That smoothes the waters? That causes the paraplegic to stand before his supporters?

Will he use the voice that frees the caged bird that whistles out of sight, though we continue to hear his greatness?

Will I ever feel loved again?

Free

Standing tall.
She felt like ending it all.
Emotions, taking over.
Felt like she was ready to fly.
Didn't question herself,
Ask if she was ready to die.
All her problems felt so big.
Greater agony of living — life in sin.

She stood on the edge,
Prepared to take the pledge.
Wind between her ears,
Felt like conquering one last fear.
It was all happening so fast.
Heart pumping, felt stagnant.
Afraid to make one false move,
Standing on the edge of the roof.
The freedom was her proof.
Become one with nature.
Feel the earth, beneath her wings.
All she wanted was to be free.

CONFESS IT IN TEARFUL VOICES

Didn't Know

Didn't know that I was sad.
Until —I started crying.
Don't ask what's wrong,
Don't want to start lying.

My heart just hurts,
Can't fill the void.

Think I lost too much.

Lord, please give them back!

Can't help but ask, hope the emptiness will pass.

Who'd you leave for me, if you took them all?

They belonged to me.

Ashamed

Tried hard to be there.
Never wanted my kids to feel as if I didn't care.
Wanted to see them,
But I was afraid of their eyes.

Yearned to hug them,
Longed to look into the skies.
It hurt to see their tears,
Wiped away my eyes.

Drove to their city,
Could never go inside.

Ashamed.

Bit my lips to keep from calling.
Tried to forget.
Continued falling.
Wanted you to know that I owe you, my life.

The guilt grows and builds.
This can't be right.
Love you all so much.
Afraid you don't love me still.

Ashamed to face the past, but it's all so real.

Why do they always leave me?

Why do they always leave me?
Couldn't even pack his bags.
In a rush — to please me.

Years go by and he passes on,
Leaving me all alone.
I mourn for him.
Cry myself to sleep.

Dangerous liaisons.
I hear his footsteps creak.
Doors slam, cars drive by,
None here to help me,
Someone tell me why?

My heart is heavy.
Temples hurt, eyes swollen.
When will it work?
Each room is a reminder of you.
My love, my provider, my life.
All I know is the life I had.

Days seem long. Can't help but feel sad.
The dreams I've earned, the husband I've known.
The things I've earned, lessons learned.

People go on around me,
They're not concerned.
I live alone, no place to turn.

Why do they always leave me?

I must let it burn.

Spiritual barriers broken.
"I love you" were the last words spoken.
Memories are my only token.

I continue to go on, by the grace of God.
Time goes on, makes me feel odd.
As I go on, I carry you with me.
Can't stop surviving.
Can't stop witnessing.
Thoughts break me down,
Now that no one is around.
Still I stand broken and proud.
Makes me wanna scream out loud.

Why do they always leave me?

I ask myself again.
Not sure why they left me,
I try not to live in sin.
I must make right with God before he takes me back
Memories of heartache and pain makes me go insane.

Until we meet again.
I must dwell here and represent.
I envision your face, features you have.
I think of old times, walk around and I laugh.
Pray to God that I can reach my predestined path.
God please wait for me,
You're the only one who hasn't left me.

Forever

Forever in your debt.
Forever in your shadow.
You've already won half the battle.
Never will I forsake you.
Don't ever plan to hurt you.
Emotions under control.
I still want you.
Can't live for you.
Afraid to abuse you…
On my knees at night—
Praying that I'd never lose you.

You dwell in my heart.
Stay on my mind.
We connect, our souls intertwine.

I cried

Today I cried,
Tried, to hold it in.
Tears kept on falling,
There was no end.
I sobbed and I wept.
Let go of the pain.
Today I cried. I hope to cry again.

TO BATHE MY SOUL IN MUDDY WATERS

The Candle

There is a candle that will always flicker at the very mention of your name. The shadows sometimes come together to create a tall image of your strong physique.

I say things and anticipate your response in my mind and I laugh the way we once laughed together. I am sure that you are still here.

You may become frustrated as I sniff at your shirts, lie on your side of the bed and use your things.

These are my ways of keeping you close. I know you are still pressured to use them as you have transitioned to the other side.

The light that flickers in the day often glows in the night. That is when I need you most.

I can hear you asking me what's for dinner, planning to go to the gym, and forcing yourself to get up two hours early to go running.

I still hear you calling for me to see a funny video or listen to a silly story while we are watching our favorite shows and discussing our day.

The candle never goes out. There are so many constant reminders that I must face daily.

The faces of our children speak volumes as I can see your eyes staring back at me in their small faces.

Different shades and ages of the father who enjoyed Sundays in front of the TV set while talking football stats and hollering plays.

The father, who on weekends would plan a family outing and surprise the kids with a prepared dinner and a movie, or lunch at a buffet followed by a good run later.

The light never dims as your voice still echoes throughout our home.

I can remember the day that we were in escrow. How you claimed it! This was only the beginning for us. This was to be our first home.

That we would have —more.

It was a testament of hard work and faith.

We both knew that with all that we were challenged with, we made it together.

The glow in our room… It seems that the room widens with this illuminating brightness.

When I feel alone is the only time that I feel this sort of glow.

As it bounces off the walls,

It's a comfort that creates more, quiet.

This glow allows me to speak freely and look around.

It's a dominant glow that helps me recognize what we shared more than ever.

I shall raise a glass and celebrate the life of the candle that will always remain lit.

Dark man

Onto his death…
I hold on to his every breath.
Dark man of the grave he rests.
A strong soul, nevertheless.
A soldiers' voice speaking with his lightly woven uniform canvassed around him.

His collar folded neatly under his chin.

I can still remember the pointed tips and the odd slants of his ears.

Remembering the realness in his eyes. It reminds me of the soft timid skies.

He was a great reflection of the love — that God has for me, and I love him deeply.

I remain alone, left with many untold stories, questions and words that I have yet an opportunity to say. Unable to comprehend as to why I feel this way.

Sorry that he left when we had so many plans. I have made peace with the facts and I am happy you traveled to the brighter side.

You remain in my heart.

Dark man you are alive!

Stain

Drive in center lane.
Absorb all the pain.
Close my eyes as I strain.
Wipe the surface to remove the stain.

The beauty of a lie

I hold out my hand to touch you.
Can't reach you.
Instead you touch my heart.
I try to summon you so I close my eyes,
Yet you are somewhere far away.
Flowers have fallen from the trees as they sway.
I feel them reaching an end.
My physical body became aware of my spiritual body and we
    committed to one another.
That's when I was able to feel you.

LOVE IS LIBERATING....

His Smile

His smile waits for a response.

The shine of his teeth, speak to whoever faces them.

Darkness is left behind him.

Tears dry into loose strips of despair,

For they are non-existent when he is around.

His smile lifts the most shaken spirit.

His smile says a lot,

His smile screams to me,

Can you hear it?

My Flower

She is my flower,
Blooming out of the crack in the rough soil.
She reaches the earth,
How the pavement opens for her entry.
She seems to direct me.
The earth never knew how to appreciate her.
Her spirit is too powerful.
She's colorful, wise and real.
I cannot draw her.
She is so complex.
I drink from her fountain,
Until there's nothing left.
I speak with her,
She never loses a breath.
She listens, answers my questions.
Gods grace renews her.
He graces her every step.

Heart

Inaccessible to touch.

Hard to escape its grasp,
It has other functions, nothing loose in its path.
No plan could be devised,
No warrior can win this war.

Forever it hurts,
Mercy understands no more.
It continues to hang on,
Refusing to let go.

The heart pumps for survival,
Beats for the arrival.
Never—does it let go.

Poetic, mechanical, written like words.
In the bible, this organ, this machine controls all.
The heart takes over my chest.
More sensitive than my breasts,
It continues to pump as I rest.

His

I've seen it in his eyes,
Through him, I've been to the other side.
Cried through his tears,
Lived in his years.
Been warm, in his embrace.
Felt comfort, in his face.
Held tight in his arms
Hypnotized from his charm.
Reborn I birthed our baby
Cradled in his nest,
Tranquil in his chest.
I speak through his breath,
I will love him until, there's nothing left.

Love It

Love it.
Grab it. Take hold. Fight to keep it.
Only you can understand. Don't give it away.
It's only safe in your hands.
Guard it, treat it with respect.

Be careful and never neglect.
Don't be naïve or do what you will regret.
Treat it as if it's pure.
The most expensive gold.

It will remain precious-
Tell a story, carry your heavy load.
It's a well-written lyric, the speaker box
That allows you to hear it.
It's the bank account that will never lose funds.
It's a part of you that has just begun.
It's an opportunity to identify all things that are good.

It's the creation that is never understood.
Do what you must,
But remember that you are one of us.
Your struggle is ours, together, we cant be touched.

Friend

Wherever you are,
You are deep within me,
In my heart,
In my dreams, in my mind and inside the depths of my soul.

I hold you within, under my skin.
Beyond my darkest thoughts.

You are the artist, sculpting the mold of my dreams.
You are the face, the resolution,
The answer to things.

Family

Family
More than family…,
You were my friend.

Nights were stayed awake taking, with no end.
Agreed with one another, almost all the time.
Time is the only distance between us.
You're always on my mind.

I'm so proud to be chosen by you.
We would think similar due to experiences we've been
 through.

Its deep how you call when I'm picking up the phone.
How I reminisce and think back to things you would often do.

We'd talk one another out of trouble.
Share our dreams, goals; plan amazing things we would do.

We are apart; I'm a little further from your reach,
You know I always return.
Things will be better.

Don't forget that our bond is strong.
I close my eyes to feel you breeze past me in large gusts of
 wind as it howls and it moans.
So much more than family how I laugh as I see your face.
You still visit time after time and it helps me remain strong.

Grandma

I miss you grandma.
Wish I could physically touch you.
I'm older now.
Wish I could do more for you.
Close my eyes and picture myself at home.
Call out to you, when I wake up alone.

So sorry that we're apart.
Conscious that your spirit is close.
Hear your voice in my heart.

Made phone calls today, wrote memos, checked the mail.

Completed my duties and still couldn't reach you.

I miss you grandma.

Imagine your smile, your understanding heart, your unselfish ways.

Been a while since I saw you.
How things have changed.

Words serve you no justice.

As I scurry in the dark searching for you.
My progress is proof that I'm still with you.

Gain

Solemn music played,
Exposed her precious thoughts.
Stole her false hope.
Carrying all the bags that she brought.
Her heart grew heavy.
Tears drove out all the pain.
She smiled at adversity
For she knew what she'd gain.

Man

Impressed by so many things that you've said.
Can't pretend that your energy isn't alive in my head.
Long for your thoughts, to connect with my own.
Beautiful secrets we share while alone.
A glance in your eyes and I reach your soul.
You are a beautiful man, whom stories are told.

Infatuated. Not sure how to give up.
Your character is so strong.
Can't do much, but hold on.
Your mind is so wonderful,
It carries me along.
Curious to see why you think the way you do.
There's a purpose, in everything.
I want to learn if my purpose is still with you.

Our lives

Sacred solemn cries,
Intimacy, that our love provides.
Hold me close,
Keep me near,
Arise without fear.
Your sensitivity.
Your seduction.
I can't go on, without my emotions.
Your sweet breath.
The sound of your voice,
Your suckle lips,
Make me rejoice.

I continue to love you.
Stand true to you.
I imagine you near, when I'm alone and blue.
Forever seems so simple.
It's easy to love you.
There's only one who could identify my mental.

Your inner being has become one with mine.
I'm prepared to be with you faithfully,
For the rest, of our lives.

Love is like the sea

Love is like the sea,
Deep and permanent,
Yet ever changing…
It has its times of fullness,
When it carries you in its flow,
Then difficult times,
When laughter ebbs…
But beneath the surface,
Love has a calm depth-
A deep caring that is always there,
A never ending source
Of strength and support…
Like the love that I feel for you.

The Rose

Two buildings sat in the center of the village.
The city of Springfield was quiet and always bright.
The light shined with yellow, pink and purple clouds
    surrounding the sky. My dreams were like miracles waiting
    to happen.
The ripest strawberry grew from the shallow ground.
The cars drove dust and ruins into my windows, but not my eyes.
My clothes were proud rags, stitched with love and strength.
I sit in the center of the bedroom on the cotton filled mats and
    I think of the beauty of my garden.
The rose is beauty itself.
The climate is tough and wild but I feel its pain.
The rose grew fast and vicious from the ground and its stiff
    stem struck the weeds and made them
Fall to the earth.
I am conscious of the rose and the power that it possesses.
A cat will slyly gallop into the flowerbed and pick the ripe
    fruits that rise from the soil, but it will not touch the rose.
My position is to care for the nature that is being conceived
    and acknowledge the beauty that lies in the power of the
    rose.

Beside You

Soulful, peacefully, gracefully, we'll walk.
Your features are brightly glowing.
I follow your face without you knowing.
I love you,
I feel you, your spiritual faith.
I know that your vows are real,
As I stand beside you.
As he releases my arm a smile creeps deep and slow.
I'm sure that this day is right for us.
We will live for each other harmoniously.
I stand beside you today, until the rest of our lives.

This Race

My breath is decreasing,
My arms are getting weak.
Feels like the wind,
Is attacking my feet.

I must continue.
I run this race of life.
I try harder to win the fight.

My destination is visible,
I seek what's on the other side.
I yearn for what cannot be touched,
I am thirsty for what is inside.
 The message, the incredible place.

The molecules that gather in my space.
The atoms that I used, each breath that I take.
I can feel it all, with each step that I make.

I am excited to receive what has never been earned,
To visit places not yet discovered,
To travel a land that has no bottom,
To eat at the table of adversity and feed the weak spirits that
    my father sits before me.

How I want to use my beautiful mind.
How I want to expose the realities of my experiences.

Why am I conscience of the voices? Yet no one else can hear them.
Why can I see the clouds forming, see the shadows move?

I must continue my race, for I have everything to prove.
Not early, yet right on time.

I can accept the hearts of those outside.
Please come in, enter the heavenly door,
For I may give you his word,
But God himself will give you much more.

You must make your decision and determine your fate,

But I have to go and continue to run this race.

NOTE FROM THE AUTHOR

I wanted to share my thoughts and my expressions in hopes that my grief journey could also help someone else. Maybe a word, a phrase or a memory may connect someone else and help as they also process what they are going through. Less than six months into my grief journey I took my babies and we attended grief camp. It was something new and different that I felt we needed. It was during that experience that I was able to identify the beginning of my "new normal."

There is power in our words. Acknowledging why and how sometimes is harder than we think. The first exercise at grief camp was to stand in front of the group with your family and share with them what relative "died" then state when they died and what caused it. It sounded much

better in my head than it did realistically. I also realized that I had never used the word "died" when referring to my loved one because the word itself seemed so permanent. Hearing myself utter those words made my heart feel so heavy. In my head I had experienced peace and was able to let go of all the boulders that I had been carrying but in reality the boulders were still there but they also felt a bit lighter after sitting in a crowded room full of people who were also connected to me in a numerous amount of ways. Grief and mourning had brought us together but love, empathy and respect had made us bond. My children were bonding and allowing themselves to connect with others who had lost their father only weeks prior.

The power of letting go and muttering the words "died" stating why and allowing me to speak his name alongside all this. It hurt but I was proud that I was able to do it. I had been connected to him for so many years that it was hard for me to acknowledge his absence. I wanted his things to remain intact, as he had left them. I needed to keep the phone on. Smell his shirts, purchase all his favorite foods and snacks the way I had been doing for the past 12 years and I would continue to refer to him in the present when I mentioned his name because it made me feel better. If I did refer to him dying I would say that he "transitioned or passed away" but this only further confused our 2 year old who continues to ask about dad several times daily and tells me that he really misses him. For the baby to witness me using the word "died" he definitely felt my sadness and wiped my tears. Before long my babies were crying with mommy because they felt the scope of our reality in those words. They felt that I was allowing them to mourn and without saying anything, we finally started the process as a family.

ACKNOWLEDGMENTS

My Aunts DeVonia, Sheila, Gina.

My cousins : Tanya, Heaven, Raymond, Ricky and Vonshea Powell.

My siblings: CJ, Nichelle, Daphne and Ron .

Friends and extended family: Cartina Rex, Marie Mathews, Alana & Kenneth Davis, Anthony Haynes, Natalie Jackson, Lina Jang, Kandice McCullough, Kiara Washington, Yashica Smith, Chief Jesse Garcia, Ponce, Jericho Espinosa, Antoinette Wade, Terrance Chase, Ashley Williams, LaTonya Patterson, Pastor Curtis Monroe Jr., Pat Monroe, Kenneth Cotton, Omari Atkins.

The road has been rough but with support the load gets much lighter.

SHARE WITH US

We have all had to part with a loved one. If you would like to share your story or poem with millions of people around the world, go to our email address (createnoise1@gmail.com), click the header using the words "submit your story." You may be able to become a published author and also help someone at the same time.

ABOUT THE AUTHOR

Andrea Walker-Williamson, author of *Mama, Who is Jesus?* The first of a children's book series has also written for *Sable Sportsman Magazine, LOOK Magazine*, several college and university publications and currently works as a grief speaker sharing her story and encouraging others to allow them to grieve as she learned to do. Andrea was always a visual learner who created stories and she found her voice in a six-grade classroom after sharing her journal as a class assignment. She is a woman who enjoys laughter but her life was derailed after her beloved husband was fatally killed in an auto accident leaving her with four children and a world full of pain and confusion. This book of poetry is what has allowed her to gain life visually through art.

Andrea debuted as a playwright when her project, *To Tell the Truth* was selected in the 2011 NAACP theater festival. Andrea earned a Master of Science in Entertainment Business from Full Sail University; she earned a Bachelor of Arts degree in Mass Media Arts, with a minor in History from Clark Atlanta University. Andrea has over 10 years of experience working in social service positions to compliment her constant involvement in community service. She has dedicated her life to her children, to social justice issues and storytelling.

ABOUT THE ILLUSTRATOR

Eli Ziv, illustrator of the *Windows for Adventure* book series with Claudia Alexander has also worked as an illustrator on *Lies & Betrayal* by C. R. King. Ziv has worked with Andrea Williamson on *Never too Young to Dream* a fiction book for young adults. Eli currently works as a graphic designer, artist and animator in Los Angeles, California. His passion for art and animation began when he was young watching Saturday morning cartoons. His enjoyment became a career after he graduated from the Academy of Entertainment & Technology and was selected for the VFX society mentorship program. Eli's inspiration comes from his interests in mythology, classic literature and world history.

www.ingramcontent.com/pod-product-compliance
Lightning Source LLC
Chambersburg PA
CBHW061930290426
44113CB00024B/2863